Here on This Plain

JANE HOOGESTRAAT

Moon City Press

Department of English
Missouri State University
901 South National Avenue
Springfield, Missouri 65897

First Edition
Copyright © 2018 by Laurie Feiler
All rights reserved.
Published by Moon City Press, Springfield, Missouri, USA, in 2018.

Library of Congress Cataloging-in-Publication Data

Hoogestraat, Jane.
Here on this plain: poems/Jane Hoogestraat, 1959-2015
2018956693

Further Library of Congress information is available upon request.

ISBN-10: 0-913785-50-4
ISBN-13: 978-0-913785-50-8

Cover and Interior Design by Estevan Torres
Cover Art: *A Fragile Clarity* by Michelle Kingdom

Edited by Karen Craigo

Manufactured in the United States of America.

www.mooncitypress.com

Acknowledgments

Grateful acknowledgment is made to the following journals, in which some of these poems first appeared:

"Winter Stitching," *Blue Earth Review*

"That Bridge" "Discoveries," "The Pickwick Crocus," and "A Letter to Michael," *Cave Region Review*

"Advice to the Newcomer," "December Evening," "Ghost Tree," "The Spoon in the Persimmon Seed," *Elder Mountain*

"Good Luck Grass," *The Examined Life: A Literary Journal of the University of Iowa Carver School of Medicine*

"Crossing the Connecticut River" and "Ghost Hawk Lake," *Fourth River*

"Blue Moon Over Nantucket Sound," *Gingko Tree Review*

"Late Tones," *Hartskill Review*

"Alt Country," *Lake Effect*

"Report From the Island," *Martha's Vineyard Times*

"Hawthorne's Sons and Daughters," "The Scholar from Inner Mongolia Visits Missouri," *Midwestern Gothic*

"A Nocturne for Starlings," "Harvest Dust," "Late Joy, Winter," and "Missouri Waltz," *Neat*

"A Common Land," "Island Time, Aquinnah," "One More for the Upland South," and "The Work of Summer," *Potomac Review*

"Fire Weather Warning," *Red Earth Review*

"Summer's Distillation Left," *Out of Sequence: The Sonnets Remixed Issue of Upstart: A Journal of Renaissance Studies*

"In Southern Missouri" and "Before a City Returns to Prairie," *Slant*

I

II

III

I

Blue Moon Over Nantucket Sound

A season ending, dark water crossing
into island time where what matters—

off-season, time away—changes in Atlantic air.
These are the September gardens, the late rare

hydrangeas, the ferry schedule shifting
toward winter hours, fewer visitors.

What am I doing walking this Atlantic island
looking for a different life? A landscape

for remembering there is a strand
in old cloth the maker saw and then abandoned

as on a late-summer afternoon a weaver
found a warp wanting, folded an ancient loom

and told Athena not to bother with that room,
that one day there would be another.

A Summer Sound in a Summer Without End

Over the same waves, a Cessna notches a wind
current, then corrects, as a voice might catch,
right itself, an almost indistinguishable stutter.
The pilot arcs briefly over the Atlantic, practicing,
circling back to a grassy air field before climbing again.
The wing makes a slight dip in the same place each time,
a riffle in a sail that won't flatten, a chill never shaken,
how the ocean darkens when you have looked too long
across the sunlit tide, water-light burning there
while the plane masters everything, it seems,
save the one small turn, like a gull checked by wind,
like moments in Mahler that will never resolve,
a flicker in the compass, wayfaring stories
we will live with, stories without endings, ever.

Blossoming From the Wood

Five white pitchers on the sun porch collect
night as it falls. Today near the harbor, sails
turned from white to gray, late season now,
hydrangas turn purple, gray, blossom from wood.

Colors of illness, or elegance. I would like to drape
the world in gray, fill these pitchers with new flowers.
Let us wrap ourselves in gray sails, glide between worlds,
silver glances carrying the there, the not there.

I will save a silver cloak for you, to wrap safely around
your shoulders. Last night, I imagined winding a sail,
not a shroud, but something almost tribal, woven
of dream-stuff, Atlantic air, the long bells at noon.

Island Time, Aquinnah

Nantucket still extinct. Aquinnah, land under the hill,
praying town, clan of the Wampanoag, eastern people
of the dawn. Squibnocket Pond the place of the red cliff-bank,
white cliffs stained, tribal lore, with blood of whales.

From the red cliffs of Aquinnah, a fragment of shell
salmon-tinged, edged with a hint of dusk, distance
on the face of things. A coast where a rock seems animate
like an imagined swimmer, a fin surfacing gray,

deceptive, until it opens a nick of sand, a reflecting pool.
Three-sided Atlantic backed by grassy plains, bluestem,
forests disappearing over retreating figures,
dream weavers slipping the net's underside.

Easy to imagine ancient spirits, keepers of time
beyond time. Early ones arriving on an ice floe
and gazing at cliffs carved by a hundred million years
might have looked up and called it good.

Now a scent of sweet goldenrod mingles
with exhaust fumes, sickly buses, skittish
over red roads. Fall evenings, sea lavender
lights the coast of native time.

Late Tones

Three round stones balance a boulder,
its hollowed-out top holding white pebbles.

I have righted a fallen planter, saving what I could,
all any day really asks. When the 11:05 angel naps

and God remains among us only as music,
cadences mend the heart in breaking it.

Brahms' *Violin Sonata in D minor* drifts its smoky
adagio across the slate afternoon, the piano

adding 3s against 2s, hint of humorous intellect,
settling back as if to say it is possible to live

too long with an ideal. That time is ending now,
but let us speak of it with kindness.

September Weather We Have Been Waiting For

How well this element suits us, human touches
left—a sagging volleyball net, edges of court
marked with yellow cord; red horseshoes, stakes rusting;
a child's plastic chair, a larger wooden one;
a compound of sand castles where a retriever plays.

One great eye an island. On the horizon today
two silver lines divide the Atlantic from the sky
as though there were another island, a field of ice
inaccessible, moving forward and away, barrier
dreams that rise at the banded limit of the view.

I have dreamt this sea, its grays and greens,
and how the silver multiplies beneath clouds,
sequins on a blue gown the singer wore,
sand the stage on which she walked, even
strands of dark seaweed, hair ribbons tossed away.

Beyond dunes and seagrasses, a lone wind turbine,
its white blades postmodern, seeming out of place
like the blue silo nearby (what on earth could be
grown so near the beach?), reminders of the made.
September weather we have been waiting for—

The Old Whaling Church

Now that Isaac (stalled inland) has cleared the Cape,
light outlines the Whaling Church, built to scale,

Leviathan sanctuary, stark cargo hold of ship
captains, bulwark in a century before radar blips

tracked storms half a continent. Different prayers—
sextant, compass, ocean charts, stars—whalers'

colors at dawn, prevailing winds the science then,
with colder currents the waves themselves owned.

The world is clean again this morning,
saltwater not turning to sand on the tongue,

the tide deepening safely around Plymouth,
though old Methodists, whalers would not approve

the festivals about to begin in Provincetown—
no need for mercy there, no water of contrition.

Hawthorne's Sons and Daughters

Here is the eastern sea, where Hawthorne summered,
where he named a confusion around the elect that remains,
a darkened lighthouse guarding a privileged harbor.

Fireworks celebrate the end of labor, tourists leave their chairs
and the first severe sky of September. Hawthorne's ancestors
dispersed toward a ribbon of the Dakotas.

What shall I say of my origins, that I grew up on a blue sliver,
a border of a now-red state, where flax in early June
forms a mirage of water that fools, momentarily,

even the farmer who planted it. That I know the ironies.
My family was busy, I tell students, settling in a new country
when Laforgue was inventing modern poetry:

I've heard of the Far West, the Prairies, life in the raw,
and my blood groaned: Would that were my fatherland! ...
Out there, I'd scalp myself of my brain from Europe.

My family didn't know about Laforgue, breaking new ground,
plowing on foot their quarter sections. Nor do my students,
Hawthorne's sons and daughters living far from the sea.

Crossing the Connecticut River

Dickinson's woods, the road she took from Holyoke, self-exiled within her own land, writing our first non-conversion narrative. We pass within a mile of her house, the plain upper room, daylilies—while the driver names the Sugar Loaf range. Landscape also of soft-spoken Jonathan Edwards, terrorizing his flock with what Dickinson was still fleeing, the Protestant dark. Muted by the time Stevens claimed the river, his dense forest allegory of tangled histories holds all the way past Greenfield. Rough syntax hews the northern edges of Mohegan land. Stevens named it a great river this side of Stygia, discounting Protestant fiction for Greek, turning from one dark myth to another, thinking to leave behind his saddening country.

A Letter to Michael

For Michael Burns (1953-2011)

I went to Providence for good enough reasons—
to work, to think, watch the city lights, listen
to the Occupy protestors drumming for peace,
the traffic on Exchange Street, Highway 1,
and to the sirens when the clubs closed.
You were in the sirens, the hard night-thoughts
about what we did with our separate grief,
the different ways we answered the question
you once asked, *What happened?*

That was one mean demon you danced with,
one lonely god you wrestled, a lesser angel
more treacherous than a quart behind the wheel
on Farm Road 93—the times you left detox,
walked most of a mile after midnight for a pint,
came back. Three times, the story goes, or maybe
that one wasn't you, but really, wouldn't a halfgallon
have made more sense? What you must have thought
you could get away with, one more dark road.

But Michael, that night in Providence,
still dark but when the sirens were gone,
someone was singing in Protestor's Park,
not drunk and you were in that song.

II

An Alternate Life

Off Navy Pier, late boats moored the harbor,
traffic curved along Lake Shore, a plane circled

Meigs (closed a decade now), tall buildings
blinking warnings. The same man scavenged

bakery trash, stared at Mother's, the bar he crashed
mid-afternoon before the after-work crowd arrived,

hip to handlers, his seat expensive then.
He was part of my city, lines of cabs on Michigan,

train windows filled with drawn faces.
And later the porch that opened on an urban

alley, where I stood breathing in a silent city
white-cold, the pre-dawn hour when I left.

Easter Falls Early

Like an early Chicago spring, wind still cold
from Lake Michigan when waves lift
the winter's ice against the breakers
and lone walkers, braced against the chill,
realize they have chosen a day too soon to be here,
Easter has fallen early this season.

So the rites seem only perfunctory,
the trees freeze again, silver over green,
individual blades of grass stand out, clear
coating to the world, while early flowers
bow in colors tinged with graying frost
and streets, though melting, make us careful.

Say we were just looking to be cold an afternoon,
listening to wind—remembering a frozen lake,
hours after dark, how ice will groan, shift
around innocuous fissures, or even break
near the shore, where some month
from now, the identical sound will signal spring.

One April years ago, I drove on Maundy Thursday
to a fork in the Missouri, sat for an afternoon to listen
for sounds of the current running through ice floes
carrying away all resistance, as though what melts
must first run hard and far, the season earning then
what this coldhearted day may yet turn toward.

Days We Would Not Have Thought to Ask For

How narrow a range these days allow,
a band of light split between lake and sky.
I've been dreaming skies again, and lakes,

often with too much light sailing across
silver, or glimmering, almost laser-like
above dark water, as though there were a rightness

to the surfaces of things. Nature forming a vacuum,
marking its edges. Another cold, sunlit room,
wind bringing rain from the river. What we dream

leaves us silent these mornings, cold squares
of light weaving among green plants,
days we would not have thought to ask for.

Linear Time

The Maori don't travel lightly, do not frame their art,
but paint with sand these landscapes where ancestral
dreamers circle the contours of a world,

and in one an American space-watching station
in Australia is incorporated as a dreamer's image.
The bright canvas with white arrows

chalked against an insular ocean opens
on a world of forms preserved and random
only for us, endless waves and not lines,

against which we read mostly the landscapes
of our divisions, and occasionally, a flash
of color that registers on a tired mind.

But for every arbitrary and imaginable reason,
we need a way of knowing when even leaving
carries grace, a healing before the night,

against an edge of all we will never know,
a certain lightness, perhaps, on a last bright afternoon
leaving a country we have traveled through.

Late Return to Chicago

I lived in Chicago most of a year before architecture stood out, before I noticed how buildings downtown provide a sense of security, of haven. Once, in a park off Dearborn, a woman filled her water container at the fountain, and then returned to a bench, cherishing the day, and I wonder if she did so every Sunday or was, like me, a visitor returning to a treasured place. I went on to a street fair, later an antique book store to buy a children's book for the son of my hosts, who are no longer together, whose son must be grown now.

Here On This Plain

III

One More for the Upland South

(After Herbert's "Vertue")

Let's do just once drive every street in this rich town,
once a country road, and learn the names of all the trees,
believe in the joy tucked around so many culs-de-sac.
A little longer this sweet day, so cool, so clam, so bright.
Let's drive around until an almost-Southern evening falls
gently across our more temperate hearts, Herbert's
seasoned timbers, his phrase for the life you have
after the world has turned to coal. Let's be his rash gazers
at all this warranted beauty. We'll make up stories
about the old houses hidden behind hedges
with ancient evergreens that droop like willows.
Even admit for a day we don't mind it
so much, just maybe, that we live here.

The Scholar From Inner Mongolia Visits Missouri

So we take her shopping in a small town, discover
"flea-market" has no translation, though jukebox, rock 'n' roll
do, old signs good background for a picture on her blog.

The scholar buys an apron, decorated for Halloween,
which also takes some explaining. We tell her about
the local Ozarks Celebration Festival, and she inquires

"Is it an important culture?" Well, probably not,
not like the Ming Dynasty, or the reign of Genghis Khan,
whose DNA is shared by more people in the world

than anyone else's, though I have to wonder exactly
how that gets analyzed. On the way home, she asks
if we can stop by the Esteé Lauder counter at the mall,

and we're game for that, swinging by Sephora first,
a chain that used to carry her brand
but doesn't anymore, so we're headed into Macy's

and while she's at the counter introducing herself
(how quaint, I think), I detour to the sale racks,
snag a pink Ralph Lauren polo, circle back and learn

our scholar has won a $200 Lauder gift bag,
and is accordingly being treated like a celebrity,
everyone working on a translation of *swag*.

Ghost Tree

At first a garbled message, *dog got it down*
over the fence, what dog I try, hear *dog came over*
the fence, dog got caught, then finally, *the dogwood*
is down over your fence. No menace there, minor
inconvenience, half the tree lost years ago to ice.
Aging toward a ghost tree, roots dissolving,
old fissure in a limb, a tree may live an extra year
or seven with almost nothing holding it in place.

When dams on the Missouri opened for a summer
past capacity, and ancient sycamores, maples stood
with river water for their roots, that was a true loss,
not this little grief, not even grief. I have not earned
most of the dark questions asked, don't mean
to claim them now. Not even a failed life, though
there were years of inattention, and I confess
to seldom having watered that little tree.

It fell across the chain-link fence, missed the wires,
the house, the better fence, and birds had long
outgrown that nest. All over town I imagine
there are chainsaws going, residents in gloves
stacking branches—pear, plum, olive—from their
neighbors' yards. Home, I'll salt the stump, wait
for burning weather, find an end-of-season sapling,
water it when I remember, and attend to other ghosts.

The Spoon in the Persimmon Seed

After he aerates the lawn, churning mud holes
for fall seeding, he says it will help with the winter
ahead, he has seen the spoon in the persimmon seed
and I have to ask. Then he says he is low country
and I don't ask, but learn a spoon means heavy snow,
while a knife predicts bitter wind, a fork mild winter.

Low country as opposed to high country, low lands
a rural world, outlands where signs speak for nature,
soothsaying an early radar? Once in Montana,
in early August, geese were flying south already,
and no one had the heart to speak of what that meant,
or thought to split a seed, read the image there.

There is a sound in the building that alerts me
when I am alone, the way a farmer checking
a corner field can tell when people have not been
around for a long time. Birds are at ease,
tall grasses not disturbed, only rabbit prints,
delicate paw markings in snow, an old deer trail.

Mountain lions are confirmed in southern Missouri,
roaming hundreds of miles from home. Locals claim
they have always been here. Panthers too. Cat dreams
thread through undergrowth, dangerous, familiar
their presence among us; what is it in us that fears
we have drawn them down from the high country?

What we can track consoles us. Here, bad weather arrives
mostly from the west, higher on the northern plains
from the east, though the farmer's barometer will catch
the change in either case, and for some, a finely tuned ear
will register a drop in pressure, a vacuum forming,
a twig about to snap, a spoon carving the persimmon.

25

In Southern Missouri

The green, the dogwood on the hills, the wild streams
seemed like paradise to those who came here,
talking of the heat in accents from the western boundaries
of the Appalachian settlement. Mountain people
who knew this was the end. Did they think
these old hills would be a corner of the world
without violence, or the last bastion
under skies as soft as these? Did they know?

Now the historical ghost chills the softer evening,
the cold fire that fear begins or becomes
before it turns into courage, or worse,
the laughter of those who know they are safe,
who know that culture, imported no less, will heal
a community so long excluded. The old dream
that poetry will make whole what nothing else
in the world will touch—that art is about feeling.

We'd rather listen to music after Brahms
and swear it makes us more gentle,
that we don't exist in their history
because they don't exist in ours—
that we, pressed, fighting late
for those we love, and thinking we were about to lose,
would not burn a house or a cross,
because we know it's not in us to do that.

December Evening

Watch with Sabbath eyes this solstice evening,
air hinting of snow, a scent of lime drifting
across a distant room, ghosts or angels unawares.
This is the time for night's homecoming, cold stars,
planets aligned, old wood fires whose sparks,
on faith, will last another short day.

There will be fires in the woods tonight, already
this afternoon woodsmoke spread over the town,
far enough south that it's still the only source
of heat for aging frame-houses, and not just those
off back roads, the edge of small towns,
the villages, as a friend from Italy calls them.

When mercury drops, we are all insular, weathering
our various exiles, waiting out the cold, watching
from doors that lead toward, toward what? The heart's
blue silence, the snow? Or other doors that lead
toward the future's appointed rooms, fires banked,
the table set for unknown guests, long awaited?

Missouri Waltz

After Jacek Frączak, printmaker

This town, near dusk, where color rings
cotton-candy streetlamps—a green, two pink,

a yellow—holds more than one might suppose.
See there on the edge, a lake, rising moon, a glow

through shades on upper floors in gray buildings.
On the deserted Main Street amazingly

a girl, a violinist, has chosen a spot to practice,
a future stretching there without malice.

Her dog waits in audience, listening
as notes drift over a steeple, follow twilight

toward the darkening green of distant bluffs.
It's an old tune, almost well-meaning enough,

whose history the violinist will learn about
in a book somewhere, look up for a moment

to remember how when she finished the tune,
a light was switched off above in a gray room.

How she realized only then that the town,
the unseen, had been listening all along.

Here On This Plain

IV

A Common Land

Though their arrowheads don't surface anymore,
Yankton Sioux once lived along the nearby river—
a genealogy of two cultures, traces of tribal language
and *Platt Deutsch* both fading, almost gone.
The harvest moon hangs taunting
a parched cloud. No romance in these fields just now.

My uncle died young working here, 1987 when
the heat baked doubt away, futures skyrocketed,
contracts were bought back. There have been good years
since then, heavy snowfalls, spring rain. But not this one:
cornstalks not worth the harvest, fissures in sloughs,
nights that breathe dry the horizon's last light.

Ghost Hawk Lake

Season of pelicans, of the lake named Ghost Hawk,
towns called Mission, St. Francis, Rosebud
of the Oglala Nation, a sovereign state
within a country. Again the medicine wheel
as a path to courage, as a path to grace.

Mainly, I go for the light over the West River
grasslands, sandstone green in June, white sage,
a changing country where the bluffs, liminal
in early morning, catch a small sense of spirit,
a bright glance filtering from an older world.

Early in the last century, one of the black-robes
catalogued three hundred plants in this county,
learned the spirit-calling songs. Lakota directions
appear on churches—red, yellow, black, white—
the medicine wheel earlier than the cross.

Fire Weather Warning

A rare alert for November, even after rain. High winds,
low humidity in the grasslands, pressure dropping—
together they chart the alarm.

The gods might be just over your shoulder when you turn,
a glimpse of something you almost catch, behind you now
a breath of sweet grass, sage, scent of bitterroot.

What of this November rain, fall crocus reblooming,
hyacinth not rooted deeply enough pushing through,
a storm forecast from the southeast? Very old,

my grandmother woke up thinking, *What will this day hold?*
Not in fear, just a curious strain for the world's oddity,
a quizzical stance, a not-misplaced bewilderment.

The winds of advent blow from north to south,
or should, but not in this season out of time,
this waiting for the unforeseen.

Against the Current

I've made this drive in a storm's island, rain light,
currents of water on the road, an overflowing Missouri
shutting the Omaha reactor down, ghostly steam absent
while new stars appeared to guide haggard-faced drivers.

Or arrived ahead of ice, treacherous lace draping
the sycamore's spine. In German, *Landschaft*
means landscape and distance, my father once explained,
to see a long way—weather approaching the fields.

But shrouded in haze, river land turns flat water
rich and dangerous. Later, golden storms drifted dust
from Kansas, and still I was driving to guide my parents
toward their deaths, not yet thinking of my own.

The Pickwick Crocus, Violet Spare-Veined

For my mother

It's spring again, sort of, mid-March, a few crocuses
blooming on the ides, looking confused, apologetic.

Once, when we were walking on campus in Chicago,
you noticed crocuses by the gothic buildings,

and downtown you said of the corridor
among tall buildings, *It's comforting, isn't it.*

I store those moments of kindness, not pretending
they came easily or often for you.

The rare dogwood my friends planted in your honor
should bloom this year. You would have liked it.

Easter is late, as when you last visited. Another dogwood
was threatened by a hard frost on that Holy Saturday

when I overheard you tell my father, *Now don't get morbid*
if the leaves go black by tomorrow morning. They didn't,

though I believe you woke in the night to check,
the season lending us an affinity for the fragile.

The Lakes of Childhood

Far inland, water laps an old dock,
a canoe on an island abandoned.

Metal signs of the resort scrape the wind,
the graze of a fishhook, the glint

of a pike's tooth. Not roads worth taking back.
It can be an act of generosity to say even that,

to let it be the last light over water, boats
motoring in, sand on the skin, coating

the oars, the dock ropes. The cabin shuttered.
There will be joy in other summers.

My Grandfather's Oranges

I.

There were oranges, always oranges
in a paper sack with nuts and stick candy,
but it was clear we should value the oranges most.

When the dictator fell in Romania, a young man wrote
an essay for the *Times* about buying his younger brother
an orange, the anticipation of that, for the brother

who had never had one. Somewhere for my grandparents
there must be other stories like that, oranges
as treasures, world of abundance, memory of scarcity.

In 1962, my young father drove halfway back across
the country, returning to his family during the Cuban
missile crisis. Many things about that year were frightening

but by the fall, that October, things were a little better,
safer, in the larger world, also.

II.

I went back to that farm this summer, though the house
has been long gone, the fields turned to sloughs,
conservation land, desolate, unfenced. Paid late
respects to the immigrant great-grandparents, their parents.
My sister almost missed the driveway, claiming the farm
did not have trees, which fifty years ago, it didn't,
though the turn is still marked by the white rock pile.

That Bridge

For my father

In the world you no longer follow, a plane has gone invisible
and commentators are saying a 777 cannot just disappear
off the planet, yet people do all the time. Driving back
after we last talked, I thought the bridge appeared
too suddenly through the fog, was just there, oddly
white, peaceful-seeming as I drove over the wide river,
the ghost bridge, the transom. Merely a headlight out, I learned
later, having driven too many miles with the brights on.

But now I hope that when your passing happens
and it will soon, will be like driving over that bridge,
a smooth transit between the night and the not there,
perhaps with snow outside, or in the flow of afternoon
light. I hope they will have read the Noon Day Prayer
because the nurse says, *He so loves the prayers.*
When the bridge appears, may it be laced with silver light,
like a good and private dream, a ghost bridge.

Good Luck Grass

He lives now near the corner of Dakota and Crow,
before the river. We have left him sweet grass

from the Lakota store, tightly woven, a blessing
for safe travels. His hands reach toward the sky,

as though he sees something there he can almost
grasp, wishes to move toward. Before every visit

I light two candles in the Catholic chapel,
though we are neither Lakota nor Catholic

and when I read him the *Nunc Dimittis*
he asks in return, *What do I do now?*

The nurse showed me where the elevator key hangs
so I bypass the code, entering and leaving freely.

I think a lot about this freedom I have
to walk through the world, drive cross-country

away from my life, take back roads over grasslands,
skirting the river Lewis and Clark charted to where

they were not expecting a tribe on the nearby island
in the Missouri, not having reserved gifts for them.

If my father lives another month or two, I'll visit again,
circle back down toward Pine Ridge later, under a sky

enormous enough, almost, to contain all longing,
landscape of loss and love, all he reaches toward.

Time and Light

For my father

A year after your death, I prune the river birches,
working first over the neighbor's roof (old courtesy)
then clearing the back yard so sun will reach
next season's daylilies, a space where
time might start again, though it has stopped so often
these years. I've hung three pink glass bottles
from the lower branches, bottles to catch bad spirits,
keep them from entering the house. By tradition,
they should be blue, and the trees cedar, but these
will do, trinkets for the furies, domestic guardians.

We scattered your ashes at the farm, near a grove
that always felt as though some event, ancient
or just beyond recent history, happened there.
Your ashes will hallow that place. You spent entire days
mowing, trimming the trees, for the family, but for many
other walkers also, we learned later. I think you may
have known that, but felt no need to advertise it, thinking
it might go better for the walkers, preserve their solitude,
your own in this almost-Grecian sacred grove,
where healing spirits rise, even now.

V

Summer's Distillation Left

After Shakespeare's Sonnet V

There is a corner of the heart where summer
is always ending, but never quite—an August evening
preserved, Dickinson's guest that would be gone,
a courteous and harrowing grace, the last bright
gladiolus blooming, the brittle lawn reseeded,
landscape being pared down, bearing that
spare look of a sadness without cause, a litany
of sameness in the days to come between the sheaves
in golden light and the driving winds of yesteryear.
Take any season you like, and what remains
will be cordial enough, if you have been careful
in your loves, and they with you. Such endings we prepare
when time seems kind, such choices we make.

Discoveries

There is a planet
        in a newly discovered galaxy
                made entirely of diamonds

that will go dark one day
        never having heard
                even an unearthly echo.

Our music will not have reached there
        nor the night owl's cry
                nor any wisdom

nor the sound of a voice
        thrown across the park in a small city
                another owl answering then

yet many lives are tethered
        I believe in the ether
                by filaments invisible and strong.

A Nocturne for Starlings

Mozart kept one, taught it melody,
and mimicked from it a line or two,
the song of one caged, not seven.

Drawn by heat from the winter city, five million
have flown in Rome near sunset,
each shadowing seven others, wings iridescent

over domes, air currents gilded, made visible.
And when the falcon is hunting prey
the formations tighten, fifty or a hundred

wound in a single, erratic ball plunging low
toward the ground to fool the raptor, which is how
the wreck happened at a Midwest crossroad,

a small pickup scattering carnage at dusk
otherworldly so many birds dead at once.
Now there are parallels everywhere, shadowy

figures in the landscape. Was the falcon puzzled
as any human sleuth? In what key do starlings sing,
the one or two who swerved that day?

Alt Country

How in Steve Earl's music you smell the dust,
Texas in August, lawns long ago crisped,

a permanent *Vacancy* sign rattling in the wind,
an abandoned movie theater, stale taste

of time so old you could still smoke there,
dry headache lasting all day, red hibiscus

cloying afternoon glare, 104 degrees at 3:13,
I-35 unrolling an emptiness you thought

to leave behind years ago, some part of a soul
you pawned knowing you would not return,

afternoons that come October you will not
be wishing back, not like that, ever.

Harvest Dust

Rising from gardens of grief,
        harvest dust clouds the horizon.

If you turned, you would see motes
        as in front of an old projector.

Turn again, and the film is still gray,
        eyecream for the dark, false choices.

The ceilings of the old theater have been restored
        in period green and gold, 1919 lamps.

It is all beautiful and grand.
        Aesthetic estrangement often is.

Winter Stitching

Strands of magenta, spring green, pastime
embroidered during a long winter folded
away in a cedarchest somewhere and lost now
like the light caught by *bromeliad, coleus,*
the flowers I tend now, strange, unpoetic terms,
odd seasons, as if beauty should speak,
dappled apple, kiwi fern, dark star, dark heart.

How to explain beauty here winding toward
spring light among what my friend calls
the *wandering jewel,* sparing me the Latin.
And the newest, *Persian shield,*
imported from a more tropical place,
rare, precious in its own right this year
of new names for almost everything.

What Matters

There is a limit for everyone
        on the number of summers
                when the first firefly appears

What matters shifts
          images   the super ego
                                performances

old loves   their ghosts   even now their shades
           who mattered the most
               and when

the size of the inner circle
          the place of mystery   intuition
                I who have lived so thoroughly

believing language   constructs everything
        learn   late   not everything can be read.

Here On This Plain

VI

Casa Blanca Lilies for the Moon

"Do not give yourself over to sorrow, and do not distress yourself deliberately."
—Sirach 30:21

Lilies the colors of sunset, Casa Blanca
for the moon. On summer's longest day
the patient was wheeled to the patio.

Some things the world cannot mirror,
the real, beyond the traces of unspoken grief,
the death of stars, registers of gratitude.

But moths return to lavender, circle
the small and lovely moments of morning.
These are the hours, the images we have.

Far enough south the city seems overgrown
when the rains arrive, river birches shade
the yard, roof, the neighbors on both sides.

Pruning a vine from the house next door
that overhangs a fence, I discover a rope
to their gate looped through my fence, call it even.

Once near San Diego, I watched a gardener so
precise he worked only with manicure scissors.
When the evening cools, summer tipping

between idyllic and dangerous, I'll be in Sirach's
vineyard again, trimming the hedge, leaving
more than twinges of the fallible, untidy twigs.

Heirloom Hostas

I have sprinkled red lava rock around the bed
of green hostas, some of which are heirlooms
from the thirties, when the plants were dear.

There are gifts one cannot refuse,
though I will ask the donor to help identify
which are old, which new, look up elephant

ears in a gardening catalogue, confess the rocks
are there to prevent me from weed-eating
smaller plants. All week, the rain has fallen

like an endless conversation reaching
a ragged edge, as though bad faith
were growing where it cannot be tended.

What the Place Has Come to Mean

I.

An older neighborhood, walnut, maple, closing over the street. Stretching to cure a pinched nerve, I catch a corner of sky. Later, new words—pedicle, thoracic vertebrae, compression fracture. Where is the MRI for patience? The sound of a single synapse, signal being restored, crackling, sap flowing through trees, the growth of roots. A body fighting for itself.

II.

Archeology, as though lives are layered, sedimented, storage, synaptic accents made of paperwork, dreams. The body an outer layer, sadness around the eyes or a light, too tentative, hesitant, an abiding gentleness, as when driving the green hills on the Missouri border, a haven of sorts. River birches overhanging the small prayer garden, space apart, a place where one lives.

Here on This Plain

Willows in late-afternoon light, water mirroring
seven, and a trail we will not be taking now.

In the butterfly tent, an Iraqi woman watches
a variegated Great Spangled Fritillary

flash rare gold while a granddaughter
coaxes back an Eastern Tiger Swallowtail.

We could say we know how hard Iraqi students
work, how sorry we are for the Levant.

There are extremists in our land, too,
beyond interpretation, not to be reasoned with,

a colonial history. We could talk of Arabic poetry,
gift of ancient cultures, how in a Chicago museum

we have visited golden treasures from Iraq, safer there.
We could say all that, and it would not be enough.

Riddles

In outer space, the seasons don't change.
I'm drinking green tea cultivated for emperors.

It's the middle of the night somewhere tomorrow,
and the soul is keeping its own time.

In the real tomorrow I may go for a walk in the park,
one I've visited now for twenty-five years.

There are details of the gardens I haven't seen,
a museum I visit once a year or so.

The students down the street are spilling out
into their yard again, and I've told them they're fine.

The ball they retrieve from my front lawn
narrowly missed the transformer, rippling the wires.

Let the heart have its own time zone set
permanently on exile. Honor the rituals.

In my tradition, if you act as though
you have faith, it will be given to you.

Before a City Returns to Prairie

It's an uneven place, between university and park,
yards scattered with stone ornaments, remnants
of gardens once cared for, a house or two abandoned
or occupied by a hoarder. From the street it's hard to tell.

Every morning like clockwork, two freeze-dried hippies
walk a tiny dog by the house and throw my paper
closer to the door. A young runner with a limp
jogs through the neighborhood, stops at the café nearby

and talks to pictures, but he always pays, and the servers
have learned to let him be. And once they asked
if I was a morning person—in the height of summer
they had been admiring my lilies on their way to work.

By accident, I own the nicest house on the block,
which others pointed out before I paid attention.
My block looks better these years, and some part
of that is mine, an influence on the minutest level

in a community of sorts, the student next door with her Benz,
home owners here and there, the young all around us
who will leave in a year or two but remember fondly
these old bungalows, their thirties charm not quite bohemian.

Half of Detroit, where I have never been, is returning to prairie,
and on some blocks only a house or two remains, welltended,
a swathe mowed, a railing repaired, a fence painted though
it divides no yard, tall grass a boundary on the other side.

Last week I repaired the front porch, or rather
an unemployed man did, careful in figuring costs
for the frame, the tools, the concrete he would need.
It took too long to dry, but he stayed into the evening.

Later a friend who works in real estate asked if
I had designed it myself, thinking perhaps she had
unearthed my hidden talent for architecture. But no,
the sketches were his, the first concrete job he had ever

done alone, he confessed, pointing out errors,
taking the money apologetically. His girlfriend tells
me he posted a picture of his work on Facebook,
that it was good for his confidence, that things even out.

Late Joy, Winter

I.

For days I've thought about stone bridges
and of Albinoni's lighter adagios,
Concerto One not announcing the soul
has closed a door, life reduced the heart
to stone, more like taking the long way
home over the beautiful, repaired bridges.

II.

An interior lit by red carnations in winter
welcoming conversation or music,
neither bright nor dark, all the seasons ask of us
action deliberate, responsible. Not a world
without pain, but one where something shines
around the edges, a room where one listens.

III.

For years I misread Dickinson's "After Great Pain"
as grief, not pain. Also, winter in the room
mid-November, the cold setting in. I've built a fire,
cleaned out the attic, shoveled the ice on the walks,
caught a cold, canceled lunch for next year,
sent off a package of family pictures.

IV.

There are more stone bridges than I realized,
WPA projects rerouting creeks around
urban green trails, winding a magical kingdom,
a newer world there for the discovering.
Later, other parks with stones built by caves
one might explore, a world made of limestone.

V.

A muted obsession with stonework. Pretending not
to participate in grief until you open the door
and find yourself in an empty hall, finally present.
Today I bought a lamp for the upstairs room, thought
of how once my sister said of a shooter he must have
been collecting slights, but I heard collecting lights.

VI.

Keep the dangerous moods temporary, a short spin
on ice, a trip into a ditch with the car turned around.
Knives that flash will flash quickly and bright. Notice
without dwelling. Hold no liens, only your own failures
as antidote against bitterness in winter, knowing how
many years the world tipped its mercy toward you.

Also by Jane Hoogestraat

Border States (BkMk Press, 2014—Winner, John Ciardi Award)

Harvesting All Night (Chapbook—Winner, Finishing Line Open Competition, 2009)

Winnowing Out Our Souls (Chapbook, 2007)

The Missouri Authors Series

CPSIA information can be obtained
at www.ICGtesting.com
Printed in the USA
FFHW02n1729061018
48673937-52677FF